Wayne's Box

John Prater

CAMBRIDGE
UNIVERSITY PRESS

Wayne found a big box.
He opened it.

Inside, there was a bear with a hat!
"Hello, Wayne," she said.

"Put on this magic hat," said the bear.

"Shut your eyes and make a wish."
Wayne wished he could fly.

They jumped up high and

they flew round the room.

They ran up the walls and

they ran across the ceiling.

They jumped through the wall and

they jumped back again.

They flew round the room on the chairs.

Then they felt tired.

The bear jumped back into the box.
"I have to go now," she said.

Wayne said goodbye to the bear.

Mum came in. "Let's go for a run, Wayne," she said.